Verses of Vulnerability

Poems of Solitude, Struggle, and Self-Discovery

Vidit Kumar

To the silent echoes of my soul,

and to those who have walked beside me,

whether they stayed or chose different paths.

To the ones who loved, left, and shaped me,

and to those who wrestle with their own solitude.

May these verses find their way to your heart,

reminding you that, in our solitude,

we are never truly alone.

Acknowledgement

This book would not exist without the people and experiences that have left an indelible mark on my soul. To those who crossed my path—friends, family, and strangers alike—thank you for the lessons, the love, and even the pain. Each of you has contributed to the person I am today and to the words on these pages.

To the ones who stayed, thank you for your unwavering support. Your presence has been my anchor. And to those who left, your absence has taught me resilience and self-reliance in ways I never imagined.

I also want to extend my gratitude to those who provided comfort and counsel in my darkest hours. You helped me uncover hope and strength within myself when I needed it most. To my mentors and peers, thank you for fostering my growth and creativity, even when my path seemed uncertain.

Finally, to every reader who opens this book—thank you for taking the time to journey through these words. May these poems resonate with you and perhaps offer solace in the quiet spaces between. In sharing this work, I am reminded that none of us are truly alone.

And at last, to the voice within me that has always existed in a form of creative energy, which has made its mark in these words. You stayed with me through both regular and rough times, urging me to write. Without your perseverance and calm determination, this book would never come into existence.

Preface

Life has a way of speaking to us—sometimes in whispers, sometimes in storms. It challenges, breaks, and molds us in ways we never anticipated. My journey has been anything but linear, shaped by love, loss, moments of self-doubt, and eventual self-discovery.

The poems in this collection are drawn from my battles with solitude, depression, anxiety, and the ongoing quest for self-respect. They capture the moments when the world felt either too much or not enough, and the times when, against all odds, I found peace in the silence.

This book is not merely a collection of words; it is a testament to resilience. It is an offering to anyone who has felt isolated in their struggles or weighed down by pain. Through these verses, I hope to reach others who are searching for understanding, and to remind them that even in the darkest moments, there is a quiet beauty in vulnerability and in our shared humanity.

Each poem is a piece of my heart, a fragment of my journey. May these whispers find a home within you and resonate in the quiet corners of your soul.

The Ghost in the House

You lived here,
But never lived at all.
A specter woven into the walls,
The father I tiptoed around,
Afraid of waking your wrath,
A tempest lurking beneath your silence.

Your presence—
Not a weight, but a void.
A shadow that swallowed every light.
We learned early how to disappear:
Melt into corners,
Feign sleep like corpses
In beds colder than stone tombs.

Perfection was your altar,
And we, the sacrifices.
An open book, a crooked slipper,
A single word out of place—
Sins punishable by fire.
Mom bore the worst of it,
Her hands blistered, her back bent,

Cooking midnight meals for your faceless
scavengers.
Her exhaustion a currency you spent
With the indifference of the blind and deaf.

To me, you were never "father."
Bhaisahab, the void's cruel echo.
Grand mother became my refuge,
Your brothers, my salvation.
You? A ghost whose touch
Chilled my blood to its marrow.

You didn't know me—
Not my thoughts, not my dreams,
Only my sins,
Small failures you carved into my skin.
The report card,
A death warrant you executed without mercy.
Even your sleep was haunted,
Muttering curses like venom into the night.
"Not good enough. Not enough."
The words seeped through me,
Slow and corrosive, like acid on stone.

Hatred grew in me,

Twisted, blooming black.
I swore that one day,
I'd face you,
Unleash years of anguish at your feet.
But life had its way with you first.
You fell—
Bankrupt, shattered,
A hollowed-out husk of the man I feared.

How do you hate ruins?
How do you rage against dust?
I carried your ghosts,
A legacy of chains.
I swore my children would be free,
Would not inherit the bruises
Branded onto my soul.

Yet here I am,
A reflection of your shadow.
Broken homes,
Children who know me as whispers,
Fatherhood—a foreign land
I am unworthy to enter.

You failed, and so have I.

Two men, staring across a chasm
Neither can bridge.
We meet, and it is nothing—
Two ghosts in the house,
Weightless, formless,
Bound only by absence.

Where Childhood Died

In the narrow lanes of childhood, shadows
grow,
where secrets fester and no winds blow.
A home with walls, but no refuge inside,
only the echoes of shame I learned to hide.

The air was thick with what no one would say,
and I—a child—was thrown in the fray.
Eyes too young to witness what they caught,
innocence splintered by lessons never sought.

A woman bathing under a careless sun,
her skin glistening where no shame could run.
Through cracks in the world, I glimpsed too
much,
the accidental sting of an uninvited touch.

Knocks unmade, doors left ajar,
a body exposed became my scar.
And in the night, a stranger's hand,
pulled me into a realm I couldn't understand.

Her laughter rang like a haunting hymn,
as she undid herself, limb by limb.
"Touch," she said, but I froze in the dark,
my childhood devoured by her cruel spark.

Cousins with smiles that hid their intent,
pulling, prying where no trust was meant.
Bodies— a puzzle I didn't want to know,
hands trespassing where love shouldn't go.

A world without boundaries, no lines to defend,
left me confused where safety should mend.
Each scene a brand, searing into my mind,
leaving wounds too raw, too unkind.

I watched love in its most grotesque shape,
a silent spectator, with no escape.
The act of creation turned violent and bare,
and I was the ghost trapped, always there.

Even the earth betrayed with its open embrace,
women defecating in a shameless space.
Nature itself seemed complicit in the pain,

as I watched, unable to look away again.

And the crowd laughed as they yanked at me,
my shorts pulled down for all to see.
Mockery danced where dignity fell,
a child locked inside his private hell.

No words came, no solace to find,
a house of silence bred a fractured mind.
I carried it all, the weight of the obscene,
a boy abandoned in places unseen.

I tried to speak, but the walls had ears,
and every truth was drowned in fears.
So I buried it deep, a seed in my core,
and grew into a tree that trusted no more.

Now I walk with shadows that whisper my
name,
haunted by fragments of unspoken shame.
Childhood stolen, a puzzle undone,
a boy who grew old before he'd begun.

Ashes of What Was

I scorched the roots of my family tree,
lit the path with vows turned to embers,
leaving behind the clasp of friends,
and the silent nods of siblings,
their care slipping through fingers like sand.

I chased the promise of her,
the one I thought would make me whole,
trading warmth for shadows,
and laughter for silence,
and the light of love for endless night.

Two marriages—two rings—
each a broken circle,
vows crumbling like brittle leaves,
lives unraveled in the quiet.

Fifteen years, a desert where love once
bloomed,
their voices, once so real,
now faint echoes in the void,
faces fading as I left them behind.

I had the warmth of arms,
the rough, real grip of hands—
all forsaken for something fleeting,
that was never flesh,
never breath.

The house I built from dreams
scattered like dust;
hope splintered,
collapsed beneath its own weight.

Now, I lie with the cold,
its fingers pressed to my hollow chest.
Dreams linger, sharp as shards in the dark,
but morning scatters them,
leaving me
alone with the sound
of my own breaking.

Regret rises, relentless as tides,
a flood I cannot outrun.
The One I sought was a phantom,
a cruel mirage beneath crueler skies.

No hands remain to hold,
no arms to reach.
If I could trade this silence,
this crushing solitude,
for the noise of love once ignored—
I would.

But the road moves only forward,
merciless in its advance,
leaving nothing behind to follow.

A Weighted Heart

I gave and gave, till I had nothing left,
My love, my soul, each stolen breath.
I handed you my heart, trusted you blind,
Believing you'd care, and be gentle, kind.

But you mistook my patience, my quiet grace,
Thinking I'd always stand in the same place.
You never thought that one day I'd break,
That even the deepest love has limits it can't
take.

Day after day, I gave without end,
Losing myself, just trying to mend.
My voice grew faint, buried under your needs,
While I silently crumbled, caught in these
deeds.

Then one day, my strength gave out,
I collapsed, tired of carrying this doubt.
My heart shattered, my spirit broke,
Under the weight of your tightening yoke.

You stood there, shocked at what you had
done,
Realizing too late, the damage had won.
Tears filled your eyes, but I couldn't feel,
A heart once full, now past its appeal.

Now you see, my love had its bounds,
I wasn't unbreakable, as you had found.
But you never heard the pain I hid deep,
Until the day came, when I couldn't keep.

Let this be a lesson, for those who demand,
To cherish love while it's still in your hand.
For even the strongest can crumble and fall,
And the quietest voices can silence it all.

But the cost of silence is more than we see—
A heart once brimming, now empty as the
sea.

Shadows Within

In crowded streets, a silent plea,
Behind bright smiles, hidden grief runs free.
Where laughter echoes, masks are worn,
Yet inside hearts, souls remain torn.

In homes where family's seen as all,
A silent shadow starts to call.
"Just be strong," they say in jest,
But burdened hearts find little rest.

We turn to rituals, sacred chants,
To wash away our pain's advance.
But sacred words, though wise and kind,
Can't mend the wounds carved in the mind.

A world that tells us to ignore,
Labels it weakness, nothing more.
Yet pain that lingers, unseen, untold,
Turns warmth to ice, and youth to old.

It's not a choice, nor fleeting cloud,
Depression wears its shroud so loud.

In India's heart, it's time we see,
The weight of hearts we cannot free.

Let's learn to listen, lift the veil,
To hear their story, frail and pale.
In a land of wisdom, deep and vast,
May understanding heal at last.

Echoes of the Quiet

Three-quarters of life has passed,
and here I stand—no crowd, no chorus,
just the hollow breath
of my own quiet.

Once, the world was loud with laughter,
thunderous joy spilling over,
and I stood among friends,
rooted like trees in familiar soil.
But one by one, they drifted,
their lives winding toward families and
futures,
leaving me the last bare branch.

I poured myself out, like rain,
giving until the well ran dry—
and no one thought to ask
what might remain.

Now, silence fills the rooms, thick and
shapeless,
the phone rings only

for the thin voice of need.

I stitch together the hours,
one frayed thread to the next,
keeping the mind busy, away from its own
shadows,
away from the emptiness that sits still as
stone.

Sometimes, I walk into the city's quiet glow,
a shadow among shadows,
wishing, just once,
to feel something more than the echo of my
own step.

They say every heart has its purpose,
that we're all needed somewhere.
But here I am, unclaimed—
a single note in the vast hum,
repeating itself, fading.

The Vanishing

I was a ghost long before I left,
a shadow stitched into the wallpaper,
a breath withheld between four walls
that were never mine.

She built a world with high gates,
locked me inside, called it love.
Her voice was the only language,
her mother's glare, the law.
Her brother—ah, the echo in her bones,
spoke through her lips,
whispered through my son's small mouth.

And I—I was silence.
I was the absence of a name.

Three years, no mother, no father,
no sister's voice, no brother's hand.
Only the sound of a door that never opened,
only the weight of a daughter I could not
hold.

She said I could be dangerous.
As if my hands, emptied of love,
could do more harm than the hollow
she carved into my chest.

I walked away—not strong, no, never strong—
but too weak to fight,
too thin to carry the cage anymore.

Now the clock is a cruel thing,
mocking me with empty hours.
Two years, no faces, no laughter,
just a courtroom where time drowns,
just a name on forgotten lips.

Was it right? Was it wrong?
Or was it simply survival?
Even now, my fingers hover over the dial,
knowing the answer before the call rings—
knowing she is the one who still holds the
door shut.

Clutch

I built you a shrine in my marrow,
stitched your name into my skin—
a hymn I hummed in my sleep,
a weight I carried like breath.

You were the tether, the holy wound,
the rusted nail in my ribcage.
Oh, how I held you—tight as a secret,
soft as a throat before the scream.

Then came the severing.
The air turned to ash,
your voice a phantom limb
twitching in the dark.

I bled absence in quiet rooms,
dragged my shadow through mirrors.
What was I before you?
What is left of me now?

The world whispers: release, release.
But I am all clutch, all hunger—

a thing unpeeling, unraveling,
learning the shape of alone.

The Weight of Thought

Overthinking— that heavy beast I feed every
night,
chewing on everything I should have let go,
all those *ifs* and *whys* I drag around,
an endless feast of questions that leave me
starved and hollow.

I'm stuffed with others' lives,
their words, their glances, their stories that
aren't mine,
and I keep chewing, keep swallowing,
even as I choke on things that were never
meant to sustain me.

And here I am, bent under this weight,
wanting to feel light, to cut through the
tangle,
to be rid of this sickness,
like sweeping a table of everything but what's
real,
the simple, the bare, the clear.

If I could let it go, I would.
I'd breathe again, step free, step whole,
not dragged down by ghosts I never asked for.

I want to walk unburdened,
not haunted by the noise of thoughts,
just one clear breath, one step
without carrying the weight of everyone but
me.

Let their lives be theirs.
Their shadows drift and scatter—
leaving me untouched, unbound, and alive
again.
But I keep stumbling, unseen,
as my mind ties my feet,
unable to move forward,
trapped in a loop that pulls me back.

The Wanting and the Fear

Next time you linger, waiting there,
Notice the ache, the hollow stare.
It whispers soft, yet grips so tight,
A shadow birthed from longing's light.

The ache is silent, but it grows,
A thorn that hides beneath the rose.
Its edges cut, its roots entwine,
It drinks your peace; it poisons the wine.

Desire breeds a trembling dread,
A fear of loss before it's fed.
Before the dream is even real,
It wraps you in its cold, cruel seal.

Each wish contains a quiet scream,
The weight of what could yet be seen.
And though it glimmers, bright and gold,
Its touch is harsh, its heart is cold.

The secret lies in wanting naught,

In unlearning all that we were taught.
To let the hunger die away,
And sit with stillness, come what may.

Release the need, let silence reign,
Unshackle fear, dissolve pain.
For in the void, the heart will sing,
Unbound by any earthly thing.

Then magic stirs, unseen, untold,
Life's gifts arrive, a tale unfolds.
A feast appears, unasked, unearned,
The fire of grace, unbridled, burns.

Not the promises that once seemed true,
But darker truths the wise ones knew.
The kind that dance at midnight's brink,
And pull your soul to pause and think.

So let the wanting fade to air,
And walk unbound, beyond despair.
Where time stands still, and fear is done,
And all you seek has just begun.

The Taste of Silence

When someone tells me I'm wrong,
the old urge rises, tight as a fist—
to prove my point, hurl my truth at them,
make them see what I see.

But I've noticed, the louder I get,
the less they listen,
and my words, sharp as they are,
fall flat, caught in the quiet
weight of their doubt.

So lately, when someone challenges me,
I try to sit with it,
hold my words in my mouth a little longer,
and wonder, *Could they be right?*

It's strange, letting go of needing to be right,
just sitting back, letting the silence breathe
between us, like air between stones.

I don't have to throw my thoughts like
punches,

don't have to win every time.
Instead, I lean back, listen,
see their side, even if it stings a bit,
and it changes me somehow—
makes me softer, steadier.

And even when I still believe I'm right,
there's a peace in seeing their truth, too,
in knowing I don't have to shout it down.
It's a small freedom, this quiet,
letting them speak, letting myself truly hear.

I'm not chained to being right anymore—
and in that, I'm lighter,
learning to leave the words unspoken,
unthrown.

The Still Point

The world keeps shifting,
twisting itself into something new every day,
and we're all just trying to stay on our feet,
grappling to keep pace, bending until we
almost break,
changing so fast we forget
who we were just yesterday.

They tell us to adapt, to keep moving,
to flow like water, to bend like reeds in the
storm—
and we do, we bend, we twist,
stretching ourselves thin,
trying to meet a thousand demands
from a world that won't stay still.

But underneath it all,
there's a part of me that doesn't change,
something steady, buried deep.
It's feels like an old, quiet room inside,
untouched by the rush outside,
where I can just sit,

where I just am.

It's hard to stay there, though,
hard to not get swept up,
but I'm learning that in that stillness,
there's a kind of strength, a power
that doesn't need loud voices or quick moves,
a peace that can't be shaken or pulled apart.

When I'm there,
the chaos can spin all it wants,
the world can twist itself into knots—
and I can stand in the middle of it all,
steady, grounded, unshaken.

I keep coming back to that place now,
like finding shade in an open field,
like drinking water in the desert,
and I know—
I don't have to go with the world's rush.
I can stay here, right here,
where things are calm, where I don't bend,
where I won't break.

Silencing the Blame

I put a full stop,
the moment I hear myself
blame, complain—
that slip of bitterness on my tongue,
that easy blame-game we play
when the day feels too heavy to carry.

I've seen it destroy me,
watched myself crumble,
a slow erosion from within,
just because I kept waiting
for someone else to mend
what was mine to heal.

There's a habit in us,
to search for someone to blame,
to pin our weight on any shoulder
but our own—
a habit that feels like comfort,
until it strips us bare.

But these hands are mine,

and so is this burden—
no answers lie
outside myself.
So I stop, breathe deep,
still that restless mind,
and pick up my own pieces
in the quiet I've learned to find.

A little strength, a little peace,
in the silence where blame
has no voice.

Unbinding

When they did what I never thought they
would,
what I never wished—
something shifted inside me,
a quiet wound cut by the edge
of my own expectations.

This hurt—maybe real, maybe just imagined—
sprung from holding on too tightly
to the picture I had painted,
a picture of trust and safety
I thought could never break.

But hurt has a shadow,
and in that shadow, mistrust grows,
creeping slowly into the spaces
left behind by my disappointment,
like cracks spreading on old, worn glass.

Now, I teach myself to let go,
to loosen the knots I tied within,
and lay down the weight

of what I wanted them to be.
Not for them, but for me—
for the peace that waits,
soft and steady,
when I stop carrying
the weight of hurt alone.

Awakening

Each day, the heaviness finds me,
a thick fog curling in,
filling up the quiet spaces
with shadows I never invited,
never asked to know.

I used to wonder why,
digging through old memories,
scraping at scars to find blame—
a story to tell myself,
someone else to hold responsible
for the weight I carry.

But today, I sit with it,
each feeling raw and unfiltered—
I let it come, like rain on bare earth,
no questions, no fight,
just allowing it to be.

I choose it, these feelings,
let them take shape and breathe,
no longer my enemies.

They belong to me, every sadness,
every ache and quiet regret—
pieces of me I can't cast aside.

So I stop searching for reasons,
stop holding others to blame.
Here I am, awake, fully here,
not wrapped in the comfort of excuses,
not asleep in stories of hurt.

And in this quiet acceptance,
a calm rises slowly, softly—
a glimpse of peace in letting go,
a strength in simply feeling
without needing to point fingers.

Burden of Longing

Desires rise like smoke in quiet rooms,
Filling spaces where peace once bloomed.
What we crave, we hold so tight—
But each wish turns calm to fright.

You think in things you'll find rest,
A shelter against life's endless test.
Yet every treasure we claim and clasp
Leaves us fearing what we grasp.

For all we own, we hold with aching hands,
The glitter binding like iron bands.
A peace once ours now fades away,
As wanting more becomes the price we pay.

And still, we chase—through night, through
day,
Stacking dreams on dreams, come what may.
But the weight of want bears down on the

soul,
Leaving us empty, yet never whole.

The Journey within

We seek love in faces, in words, in touch,
Hoping for warmth, yet wanting too much.
Wrapped in longing, in dreams unsaid,
We ache when love stumbles, feels distant
instead.

But what if this journey begins within,
With every scar, each place we've been?
If I learn to see myself clearly and true,
To honor the light in my own view—

Then love grows gentle, steady, and strong,
A place of peace, where I belong.
No need to cling, no need to plead,
Just resting in the joy of being freed.

And from this space, my heart overflows,
Sharing warmth wherever it goes.
The more I give, the more I gain,
A circle of joy, untouched by pain.

In learning to love the person I am,

I find a calm no loss can slam.
For love's first home is deep inside,
From there, it grows—a boundless tide.

The Dance of Forgetting and Remembering

I walk a path where shadows stretch long,
Where memories cling like the dust of the
earth—
A past so heavy, it weighs on the chest,
The echo of old wounds, old words—
The sharp sting of forgotten names.
I forget. I forget. I forget.

Time beats like a restless drum,
Tangled between what was and what is,
I forget the stillness that is my soul,
The silent pulse beneath the noise,
The ancient thread that binds me to the sky.
I grasp for meaning in the scattered pieces—
The ghost of who I once thought I was,
While the truth slips away,
Like water through the cracks of my hands.

Yet in the stillness between heartbeats,
A whisper returns—

I remember—
Not the scars that mark my skin,
Nor the voices that wound my pride,
But the deep calm that flows beneath,
The knowing that does not need to speak.

I am not my grief, nor my anger,
I am not the weight of all that has passed—
I am the fire that burns without smoke,
The quiet that hums in the spaces between
words,
The eternal dance of the soul,
Untouched by time, untouched by ego.

But oh, how the dance pulls me again,
Forgetting, remembering—
I sway between them,
Caught in the endless rhythm of the world,
And yet, in each step,
I return to myself—
The truth that I was always meant to be.

Echoes of the Unsaid

I wanted to write down exactly what I felt,
but the paper stayed empty, a hollow shell.
Ink refused to spill, afraid of the dark,
as if words themselves were fleeing the mark.

There's a chasm inside where thoughts sink
and die,
where echoes of voices pass hollow and dry.
I reach for a sentence, but it crumbles to dust,
as if my own mind has betrayed my trust.

The silence is thick, a weight in my chest,
a quiet disease that grants me no rest.
In shadows it lingers, in darkness it feeds,
a hunger that grows from unsown seeds.

I tried to write sorrow, tried to give it a name,
but the paper stayed silent, untouched by my
shame.
Empty it mocks me, as hollow as bone—
a witness, a tombstone, for what I won't own.

Alone as I came

Born in sunlight, laughter light as breath,
a childhood of gold where shadows never fell.
I dreamed without fear, saw myself on my
father's path,
no clouds on the horizon, no weight in my
steps.

But life has a way of cracking open the safe,
of wrecking what you thought would always
stay whole.
The business broke down, the riches
dissolved,
and I stood there, empty, nothing left to hold.

I stumbled through studies, drifted without
aim,
no job in sight, just failure close behind,
working dead-end shifts through the night,
clinging to my family, trying to stay alive.

I thought love might save me, tried to build a

home—
seven years spent dreaming, gone in under
one.
A marriage built on hope, shattered to dust,
and I was left holding nothing but loss.

I tried again, thinking love could heal,
but in the second go, I forgot how to feel,
lost myself, piece by piece,
until I chose to walk away, to breathe in
release.

Now my children are strangers, kept back by
time,
their laughter, their touch fading from
memory.
A year and a half—still I don't understand,
and the ache digs deeper, every single day.

I walk through this life stripped bare, alone,
fighting through silence, choking for breath.
I came into this world without a hand to
hold,
and here I am still, alone in the dark.

Yet somehow, I keep standing, though my
heart's worn thin,
searching the night for any trace of my name.
I came into this world alone... and alone, I
remain.

The Pitfalls of Comparison

In the quiet halls of reflection, where shadows quietly linger,
I find myself caught in comparison's trap,
pulling me under.
Every step I take, measured by someone else's stride,
Chasing endlessly, as peace slips further from my side.

A brief, hollow pride when I feel superior for a while,
But inferiority lurks, hiding beneath every forced smile.
Jealousy's whisper grows, feeding the ego's demand,
Caught in this cycle, my self-worth slipping from my hands.

But then, I notice the beauty in my own pace,
Embracing my path, finding pride in my

unique grace.
No longer bound by comparison's heavy
weight,
I find peace in each small step, no matter how
late.

With self-acceptance, a quiet peace settles like
a dove,
Free from burdens, my heart softens with
love.
No longer judged by the scale of another's
worth,
I walk my own journey, heart and soul set
forth.

The Virtue of Patience

In life's tapestry, patience gently threads its
way,
A calm demeanor when everything's in
disarray.
It's not just about waiting but learning to see,
The beauty in letting life flow naturally.

Being present lets us find joy in each day,
As change rolls in, with morning's quiet
display.
Patience shows us how to bend, not break,
To find the magic in every small mistake.

In the still moments, we grow and reflect,
It's in the quiet that wisdom starts to connect.
Like a river's steady course, life shapes with
grace,
And patience helps us keep up with its pace.

With each breath, we learn to release and be
free,
Embracing the journey, letting things simply

be.
For in patience, there's a beauty that shines so
bright,
A guiding light even in life's darkest night.

Where Optimism Rises

In the darkest moments, a light still glows,
Optimism flickers, even when the night grows.
In the depths of a crisis, a sign comes through,
A call to rise up, and see something new.

An optimistic heart looks past the pain,
Finding chances to grow, and start again.
Even when dreams shatter, a new day will dawn,
Turning despair into hope to carry on.

The winds of life may try to knock us down,
But resilience stays strong, pushing back with a frown.
Letting go of complaints, breaking resentment's chains,
Optimism shines, steady and remains.

Every struggle holds a gift in disguise,
A chance to stand taller, to reach for the

skies.
With optimism, locked doors swing open
wide,
Revealing new paths, where none seemed to
hide.

Through life's chaos, optimism lights the way,
Bringing hope and promise to every new day.

Addicted to Praise

In quiet admiration, we often find our joy,
A deep desire to be seen, without feeling coy.
We all want to be valued, liked, and
understood,
But in chasing approval, we must tread where
we should.

Praise is sweet, like honey to the soul,
Yet craving it too much can take its toll.
We seek validation, a never-ending flow,
Fearing that without it, our self-worth won't
grow.

But what about those moments no one ever
sees?
Can we feel proud without an audience to
please?
To give our best, without needing a cheer,
To welcome kind words, but not hold them
too near.

Let's learn to dance in the rain, without

applause,
And find joy in the journey, not in the cause.
For in giving from the heart, with no strings
attached,
We find real meaning, not a feeling
mismatched.

May we see our worth in who we truly are,
Unaffected by silence or praise from afar.

Enjoy Every Moment

In the fleeting moments of time, we shape our
fate,
Days slip away, like sand through a gate.
Each one a gift, polished by life's gentle hand,
Precious and valuable, yet often left
unplanned.

We rush through our days, blind to what's
near,
Missing the beauty that's always right here.
Life is woven from moments, simple and
small,
But unravels quickly if we don't catch them
all.

To be fully present, with each breath we take,
Is to grasp the essence of life, wide awake.
Mindfulness opens up a world so bright,
Revealing hidden treasures, often lost to
sight.

Treat each moment like it's the only one that's

true,
Where love, joy, and gratitude come into
view.
For when we're present, life's beauty is clear,
Turning simple moments into memories we
hold dear.

In the now, we find a place to rest,
Where time slows down and life feels its best.
So let's savor each hour, as it passes by,
And turn every moment into something to
live by.

The Hunger of Time

The clock is a beast that feeds,
Gnawing at the marrow of my hours.
What I touch, I nourish,
What I ignore, I starve.
But oh, the greedy hands—
What do they deserve?

I ask the hollow sky:
Who beckons today?
A task, a face, a fleeting flame—
Or the void where silence reigns?
Is it I who must choose,
Or have I already been consumed?

Attention drips like blood
From an unhealing wound.
I give, I give, and it grows—
A tangled vine, choking my veins.
How long have I knelt here,
A gardener of shadows?

Master, slave—

The roles dissolve like ash.
I wait for the world to turn its gaze,
For some echo to answer my name.
But waiting, too, is a choice—
A slow surrender, a gentle death.

And so, I ask the empty hour:
Shall I devour, or be devoured?

The Pulse of a Wreck

A single call—
A ripple through the veins,
Like a trapped bird's frantic flutter,
Its wings bruising the ribcage.
Heartbeats—a galloping herd—
Mad with purpose,
But directionless.
Twenty-four hours, they drum.
And then the silence,
Heavy as stone,
Pressing its weight into my skin.

Each moment without you
Is a stretched horizon,
A vast, empty ache.
I stumble through days
With trembling hands,
Clutching at echoes.
What use are these hands
If they cannot hold love,
If they only sculpt ruin
From what they long to protect?

I am no anchor,
Only a loose mooring,
Letting go, letting drift.
Each love slips like sand
Through a sieve of my making,
A slow erosion of everything
I once held dear.

I was the tremor,
The Faultline beneath
The homes I tried to build.
They crumbled—everyone.
I see their remnants now:
Walls hollowed by doubt,
Windows shattered by anger,
And scaffolds of promises,
Their rusted nails still
Piercing my palms.

Yet in the ruin's shadow,
A quiet moment lingers:
The day I stood in the rain,
Your voice unsteady with goodbye.
I looked to the sky,

But even the storm refused to wash me clean.
I carried it all—the ache,
The weight of your retreat—
Like a shroud, sewn into my skin.

But then—
Something stirs in the cracks.
A stubborn green sprout,
Clawing through the rubble,
Daring to rise against the decay.

Perhaps not all
Is meant to be whole.
Perhaps even the broken
Can learn to grow.
So let the pulse beat on,
Its rhythm steady, unfinished.

The river may be dry,
Its bed cracked and bare,
But the seed roots deeper still.
What is left for me now?
Only this:
A life still breathing,
A pulse daring to persist.

The Quieting

The mirror softens; its voice grows still,
no longer calling for praise.
Days drift, unbothered by applause
or the sun's gilded nod.

I stand steady—no longer leaning
on the fragile cheers of others.
The urge to prove myself dissolves,
like salt washed clean by patient rain.

Once, I shouted to be seen,
begging the world to hold my name.
Now shadows cradle it gently,
a whisper unraveling into air.

I wear silence like an old coat—
heavy, yet warm in its embrace.
Its weight no longer a burden,
but a comfort earned with time.

Kindness lingers beside me now,

its touch a balm, unhurried, calm.

I no longer chase glittering prizes,
nor crave the envy of fleeting eyes.
My mind quiets; my heart softens—
and in stillness, I bloom,
like morning mist lifting to reveal
a world I now see clearly.

The Lessons We Were Never Taught

No one taught me the art of holding myself,
of fastening the bones with wire,
of keeping the mind from unraveling
like a spool of loose thread in the dark.

They taught me history, equations, the weight
of dead kings—
but never the gravity of my own moods,
never how to leash the beast of my thoughts
before it gnawed through the walls of reason.

I wake to the clock's silver grin,
to a list of duties peeling at the edges.
Who will teach me how to carry them?
How to balance the four brittle limbs—
relationships, roles, responsibilities,
resources—
without splintering like a porcelain doll?

The mind is a wild room,
a house without doors, without exits.

Some days it is a scream in a locked drawer,
some days it is silence swallowing its tail.

And still, I must walk, must smile,
must stitch myself into the suit of
expectation,
button up the chaos, iron out the fear—
pretend I was born knowing how.

Being Comes Before Doing

In hurried steps, the world does race,
Chasing time in frantic pace.
Hands that toil, minds that scheme,
Lost in the chase of a fleeting dream.

Yet, before the task, before the stride,
There lies a space, so deep, so wide.
A quiet presence, calm and free,
A simple truth—just learn to be.

The river flows, the winds embrace,
Without a rush, without a chase.
The stars don't strive to shine so bright,
They simply are, and gift their light.

When stillness speaks, the soul can hear,
The whispers soft, the calling clear.
No need to grasp, no need to strive,
Life unfolds—aware, alive.

For peace is not a prize to win,

It rests in us, it dwells within.
And those who pause, who truly see,
Find life itself flows effortlessly.

So, let the world rush if it must,
But plant your feet in mindful trust.
Before the doing, let yourself be,
And watch life bring all that you need.